Your Easiest Route

Your Easiest Route

Peter Gilpin

Library of Congress Control Number:		2010919258
ISBN:	Hardcover	978-1-4568-4178-2
	Softcover	978-1-4568-4177-5
	Ebook	978-1-4568-4179-9

This book was printed in the United States of America.

To order additional copies of this book, contact:
Xlibris Corporation
0-800-644-6988
www.xlibrispublishing.co.uk
orders@xlibrispublishing.co.uk
301482

Contents   Page

CITY LIMITS DRIVING CENTRE

Learner Driving Manual

This book is designed to show in easy stages, the basic's of car control, intermediate lesson plans, preparing for the DSA Driving Test, and additional hints and tips once you have qualified.

By now you will probably have started your driving theory training, which in itself will assist you with the practical element of learner driver training. If not, then book onto our weekly theory training sessions. Our theory & hazard perception training is classroom based and runs on a six week revolving cycle. i.e.: if you join in week 3 and continue through weeks 4/5/6/1 and 2, this will give you all the information you require to pass your theory test.

Everything we do as a driver has a routine and procedure, which gives us our system of car control. From the moment we step into the vehicle we begin with the cockpit drill, which enables us to set up the vehicle controls to suit our individual needs. From there we move onto:

Novice

Clutch Control—Moving Off—Normal Stops—Braking Exercise—Gear Changing—Hill Starts—approaching Junctions to turn Left and Right.

Intermediate

Manoeuvres—Junctions: Y—T—Crossroads—Unmarked Junctions—Traffic Lights and Pedestrian Crossings.

Experienced

Making Progress—Avoiding undue Hesitancy

The DSA Driving Test—Pass Plus

All these topics and more will be fully covered, in an easy to follow manner.

Good Luck and Safe Driving for Life

As I said in the introduction, the first procedure is the 'cockpit drill'.

Yes, we want you to be comfortable when you are driving, but more important is the fact that you can reach both the foot and hand controls easily. To this end the 'cockpit drill' is designed to do just that.

The cockpit Drill

Doors

Now that you are in the driver's seat, it is your responsibility to make sure that **all** doors are properly secure.

For example, did you know that there is a secondary lock on all vehicle doors . . .

Try pulling the door once it has been closed. If there is any movement or rattling, then the door is not properly shut. Re-open the door and pull it towards you firmly until you are sure it is secure. **(Remember to look over your shoulder before opening any door).**

Seat

The correct position for your seat is, when you have depressed the clutch pedal (Left pedal of the three), there should still be a slight bend at your knee. To adjust your seat, place your left hand under your legs at the front of the driver's seat to locate the adjusting bar, lift or slide the bar, and with your right hand on the steering wheel for balance, you will be able to slide the seat forward or back to obtain the best position for your leg length. The head restraint should be adjusted so that the top of the restraint is at least level with your eyes (or the top of your ears) and as close to the back of your head as is comfortable.

Remember. Once you have moved the seat, check to see that you are not overstretching. Look for the bend in your knee.

Steering

Imagine that the steering wheel is a clock face. The normal position for your hands would be at TEN-to-TWO or a QUARTER to THREE. That is to say that your left hand would hold the steering wheel around the NINE or TEN position of the clock face, and your right hand would hold the steering wheel around the TWO or THREE position of the clock face. You must be able to move your hands freely all the way round the steering wheel, and to check this, place your hands on the steering wheel at the TEN to TWO positions, with your thumbs on the outer rim. You should be able to move freely from the top of the wheel to the bottom, so that your hands meet. If your elbows touch the door or seat you may have to adjust the back of the seat (The Rake), in order to let your hands move more freely.

The adjustment control is normally found on the side of your seat towards the rear. Turn clockwise to move forward, anti—clockwise to move back.

Your Instructor will inform you of the controls of his car, as different makes and models vary.

Seatbelt

The easiest method I have found in which to put on a seatbelt without dislocating my right shoulder is to stretch my left arm across my right shoulder, pull the seatbelt buckle across my body, and slot it into the anchorage point in one easy movement.

Whichever method you use, the important point is that the belt should lay flat across your body, without any folds or creases on it.

If, for example, you cause the car to stop suddenly and the seatbelt locks, the edge of the belt could dig into you and cut your clothing, or worse cut into you.

Mirrors

When learning to drive in an Instructors car you will be faced with either four or five mirrors, Your Instructor has either one or two, **you** will always have three. Which are:

Nearside (Door) **Interior** **Offside (Door)**

Interior

To set up the interior mirror you should adjust it with your left hand. (To adjust it with your right hand would bring your back off the seat and when you sit back the mirror would not be in the correct position for your new position in the seat).

Adjust the mirror so that you get the best possible view through the rear window, especially to the offside, without having to move your head.

Door Mirrors

To adjust the door mirrors properly, you should be able to glance along the side of the vehicle, with the road or pavement behind, at its furthest point away from you, should sit about half way up the mirror.

Always check the mirrors are clean and properly adjusted every time you intend to drive a vehicle, as part of your cockpit drill.

Blind spot

This is an area of road which cannot be seen in your door mirrors. To check this area you must look over your shoulder (to the right when moving off), and look behind to the area behind the vehicle not visible in your door mirror. Your instructor will point this area out for you. The cockpit drill should be performed every time you intend to drive a motor vehicle and in the order stated. I.e. if you were to adjust your mirrors and then move your seat position, the mirrors would not be correctly adjusted—if you put on your seatbelt and then tried to move your seat forward, the seatbelt would not allow you to move freely. Therefore, always use the **DSSSM** routine.

The Foot Controls

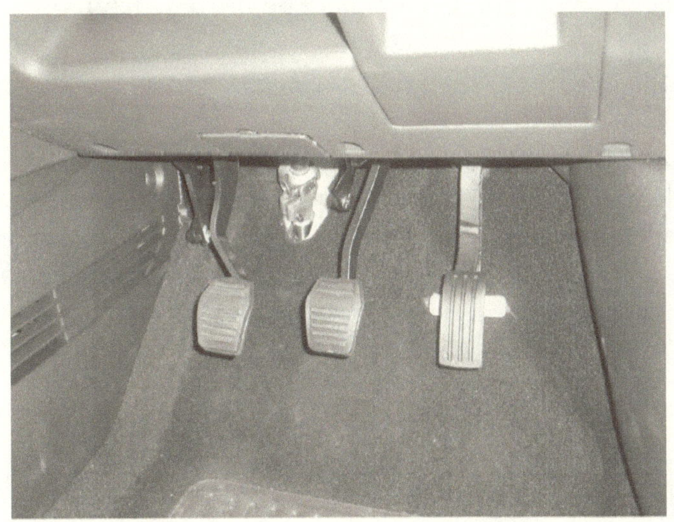

Clutch Footbrake Accelerator

Accelerator

Generally known as the GAS pedal, and used by the right foot, this pedal requires the least amount of pressure to operate. When the engine is running and you depress the GAS pedal, you simply increase the amount of fuel going into the engine, which makes the engine run faster.

This will not move the vehicle, only the clutch will do that. By making the engine run faster you create more power.

Footbrake

The footbrake (as opposed to the handbrake), operates on all four road wheels, and as this braking system operates by way of hydraulic fluid, reacts very quickly to any pressure applied to the pedal.

(Please note that this pedal should be used gently).

As with the GAS pedal, the footbrake is operated by the right foot.

The first contact to be made with this pedal before you feel the vehicle slowing down, is with a micro-switch, which causes the brake lights (red lights at the rear of the vehicle) to light up, and as such becomes a signal to other road users that you intend to slow down or stop. I will cover braking in more detail in the chapter Move Off/ Normal Stop.

The Clutch

The clutch pedal is the mechanism that allows you to engage, and change gears. The clutch transfers the power from the engine, via the gearbox, onto the road wheels to drive the vehicle.

The clutch pedal is operated by the left foot.

In diagram fig.1. You will see that both the engine and the gearbox have a plate connected to them.

In this diagram the Clutch pedal has been pressed down. When you do this, you simply separate the two plates, which disconnects the drive (Power) from the road wheels. It does not matter how fast you press the Clutch pedal down, what does matter is how fast you bring the Clutch pedal back up.

In diagram fig.2. The Clutch pedal is 'up', and when this is allowed to happen you have made the connection between the engine (Power) and the road wheels, which will drive the vehicle. If you allow the Clutch pedal to come up too quickly, you risk stalling the engine, that is to say the engine will stop running, as there is not enough power at this time for the engine to drive away even the lightest of cars immediately, you must start off slowly and gradually build up speed.

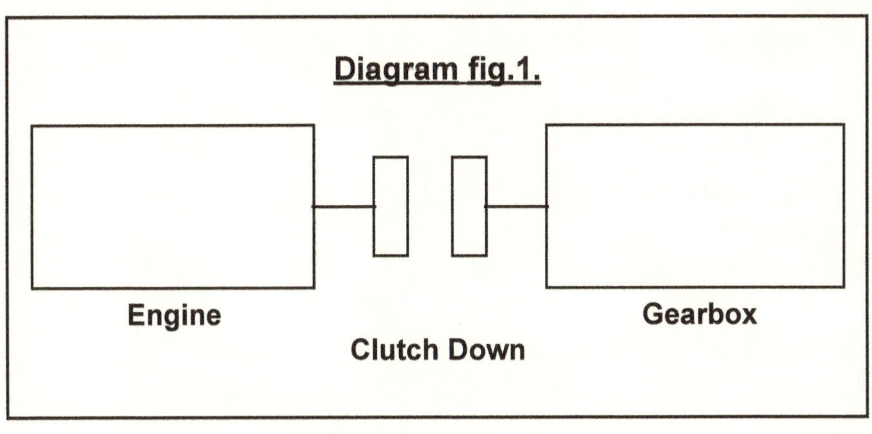

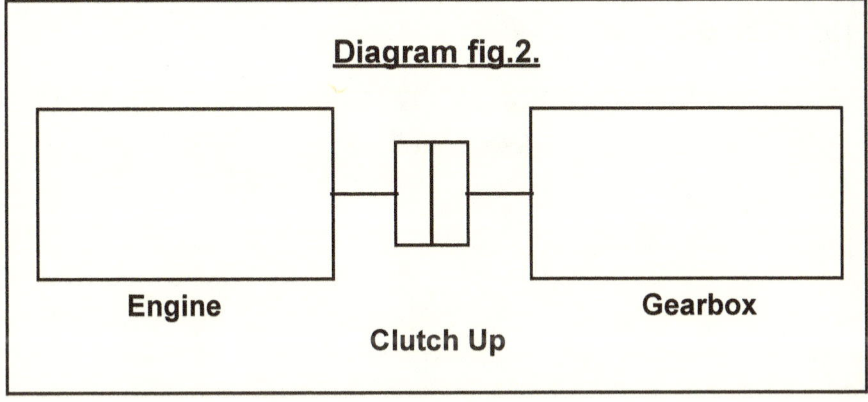

Biting Point

Biting point, is (when the engine is running and you have selected 1st gear), you slowly bring the clutch pedal up until the two plates just touch and no more.

(This is sometimes called friction point). At this point you will notice three different effects:

The engine noise will drop as it comes under load.

You will feel a slight vibration in the vehicle.

You will see the front of the vehicle rise up slightly.

When these three factors occur, this is what's known as 'Biting Point', and at this stage the vehicle is ready to move off. The handbrake is holding the vehicle stationary.

The Handbrake

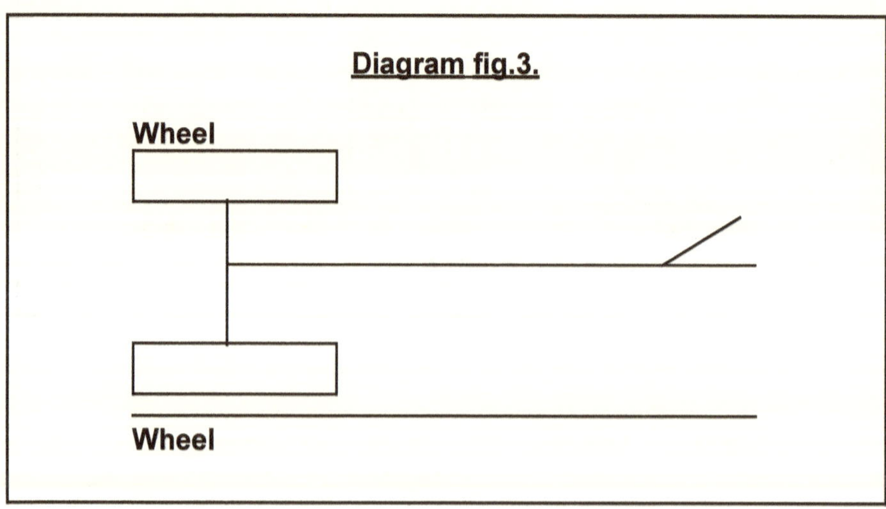

The handbrake is only operated on the rear wheels, and when it is applied, it pulls the brake shoes onto the wheel drums, which causes the wheels to lock. It is operated by way of a steel cable, which, via a ratchet within the base of the handbrake itself, runs the length of the vehicle to the brake shoes on the rear wheels.

The handbrake should only be applied when the vehicle is stationary, as to do so otherwise would lock the rear wheels causing the vehicle to skid. In the 'UP' position the handbrake has been applied. To release it, pull the lever up to take the tension on the steel cable, press the button located at the end of the handbrake (which allows the ratchet to 'fall'), and push the lever to the floor.

To apply the handbrake, press the button in (continue to press), pull the lever up until you feel the tension on the cable, release the button, and relax your grip on the handbrake.

Please note: You should always use the button when applying the handbrake, as it allows the ratchet to retract which saves wear on the steel cable. **Be car friendly!!!!**

Gears

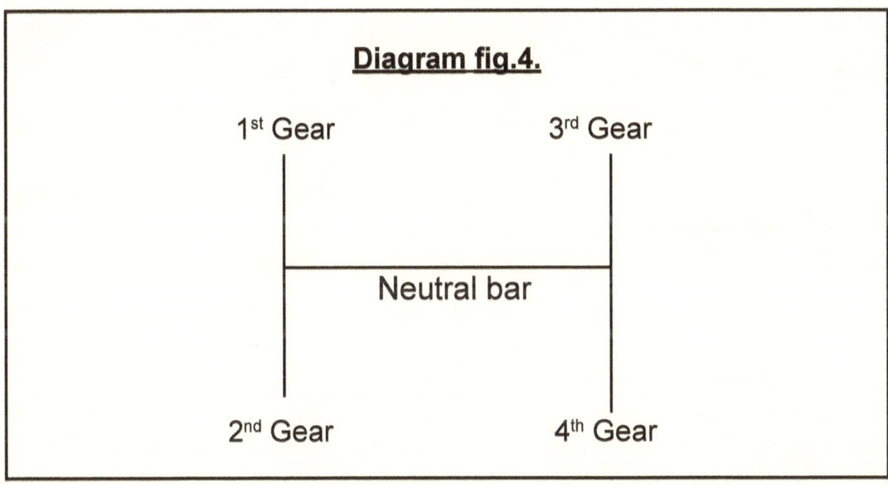

Most modern cars have five forward gears and one reverse gear; however, for the purpose of this briefing we will concentrate on the first four forward gears. Diagram fig.4, You will notice that the gears are connected by what is known as the neutral bar, and when the gear lever is in this 'neutral' position it will always sit on the neutral bar in front of gears 3 and 4, as the gear lever is spring loaded and is designed to do so.

When changing gears we use the term 'palming method', by this we mean, that as the gear lever is spring loaded to sit on the neutral bar between gears 3 and 4, it is easier to use this method (to avoid mistakes).

Put simply, to select 1st and 2nd gears the palm of your left hand should face away from you towards your instructor, pressing on the side of the gear lever (top of the lever). To select 3rd and 4th gears your palm should rest on the top of the lever.

First Gear

First gear is called the power gear as it has to move the total weight of the vehicle along with any passengers, from a stationary position. This requires a lot of power (hence the name), but will only move the vehicle at slow speeds. Any time you move off from a stationary position, generally speaking, you should use this gear.

Second Gear

To increase the speed of the vehicle you will have to select a higher gear, so you 'change up' to second gear. This gear is called a working gear, as you are making the engine and gearbox work harder in order to build up more speed. Again this gear will only allow a lower limit of speed (the higher the gear the greater the speed), so you will have to 'change up' once more to a higher gear.

Third Gear

Third gear is also called a working gear, as again you make the engine and gearbox work harder to increase the speed of the vehicle in order to achieve a suitable speed for the road or conditions that you are driving in. Let us assume that you are in a built up area, and you can safely continue at 30 miles per hour.

Fourth Gear

When you have reached your cruising speed (as above), you should then select fourth gear. This is called the cruising gear as it lets you maintain your speed without working the engine and gearbox any harder, and also allows you to gently increase your speed if the road and conditions are suitable.

Reverse Gear

Reverse gear should only be used at a slow walking pace, and you must make sure there are no pedestrians or obstructions around you when using this gear. If unsure, get out of the vehicle and look. The location of reverse gear varies depending on the make and model of your car, your instructor will advise you about the particular vehicle you are learning in.

Gear Changing Guide

Gear		Speed
First	up to	10 mph
Second	up to	20 mph
Third	up to	30 mph
Fourth		30 plus mph
Fifth	At speeds over 40 mph	

(Mph = Miles per hour)

The Ignition Key

When you insert the ignition key into the slot (generally found on the steering column), you will probably be unable to turn it, this is due to the fact that that the steering wheel has a lock which has to be released before the key will turn freely.

To do this, you will find that the steering wheel will only turn slightly in one direction, turn the wheel until there is a little amount of play on the wheel and at the same time turn the ignition key until you feel more play on the wheel (you will also hear a single click). The steering lock will now be off, and the wheel will move easier in either direction.

The next position for the ignition key (one more click), will open up the electrical circuit of the car (the ignition). When the key is in this position a row of lights are illuminated on the dashboard in front of you. Normally there are three RED lights, and as such red is treated as a warning. One of these lights will depict an oil can, which would indicate that there is no oil pressure. Once the engine has been started oil pressure will immediately build up and this light will go out.

The second RED light shows a battery symbol. This is to indicate that the battery is not being charged. Again, once the engine has been started—via a series of pulleys and fan belts connected to an alternator, an electrical charge will be sent to the battery to recharge any power used and this light will also go out.

The third light is the handbrake warning light. The symbol for this can be a circle with a small curve part way round each side, or as in some models a simple 'H'. When the handbrake is released this light will also go out. The handbrake warning light doubles up as an indication that the front brake pads are wearing down, and if this or any other RED light should come on while you are driving you must stop immediately and investigate, or seek professional assistance.

The next turn of the key (click), will start the engine. Once the engine has started, relax the pressure on the key, it is on a return spring and will return to the ignition position (2nd click), as you still require the electrical circuit to operate the lights, indicators, windscreen wipers etc.

Please note: Before starting the engine you should make sure that the handbrake is on, and the gear lever is in the neutral position.

Indicators, windscreen wipers, horn etc, are found in different locations depending on the make or model of each car. Your instructor will advise you during the cockpit drill as to their positions.

Instructions for the Foot Controls

There are four instructions for each pedal, which are:

Gas Pedal

1.	Set the gas.	(Put gentle pressure on the gas pedal with your **right** foot to increase the power).
2.	A little more gas.	(Gently increase the pressure).
3.	A little less gas.	(Relax the pressure, but not completely).
4.	off gas.	(Remove your foot from the pedal).

Foot Brake

1.	Cover the brake.	(Place your **right** foot over the foot brake pedal).
2.	Gently brake.	(Apply gentle pressure to the brake pedal).
3.	Gently brake to a halt.	(Increase the pressure, and as the car comes to a halt, ease off a little pressure to obtain a smooth stop).
4.	off brake.	(Remove your foot from the pedal).

Clutch

1.	Cover the clutch.	(Place your **left** foot over the clutch pedal).
2.	Clutch down.	(Press the clutch pedal down).
3.	Slowly clutch up.	(Slowly bring the clutch pedal up to biting point).
4.	Slowly clutch up	(Slowly remove your **left** foot from the clutch pedal). all the way.

These are the only instructions you should be given, and once memorised and understood, you will be able to follow instructions on the move.

The Moving off Procedure

POM routine

Preparation.
Clutch down (keep it down)
Select 1st gear
Set the gas
Slowly clutch up (to biting point)

Observation
All round observation
Check interior mirror
Check offside door mirror
Check your blind spot
Signal if necessary (if it would help any other road user)

Manoeuvre
Release the handbrake
Steer to safety line (1 metre from kerb)
A little more gas
Check your interior mirror

Diagram fig.5.

Preparation—Observation—Manoeuvre
P—O—M

Remember a final blind-spot check before moving off
Safety line is 1metre from kerb (3ft) or the middle of the lane you are in
Always check your interior mirror once you have moved off

The Normal Stop Procedure

MSM routine

Check interior mirror
Check nearside mirror
Signal if necessary (if it would help any other road user)
Off gas
Cover the footbrake
Cover the clutch
Gently brake

Steer slightly left towards the kerb
Clutch down; keep it down (at around 5mph)
Gently brake to a halt
Keep your feet still
Apply the handbrake, Select neutral, and Cancel any signal given
Now you can rest your feet

Diagram fig.6.

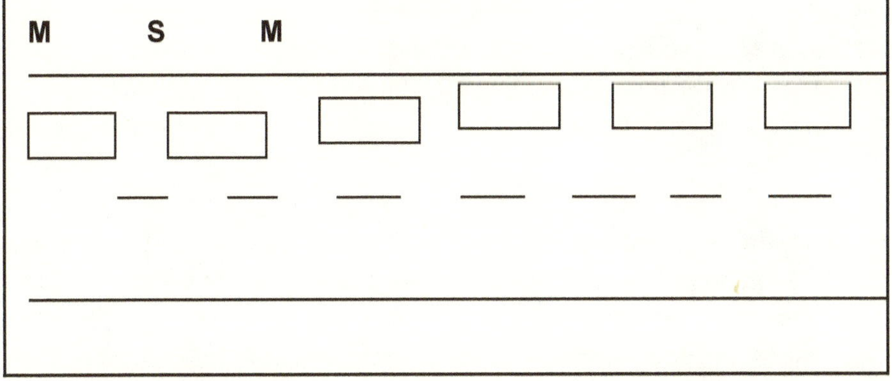

M S M

To recap, before starting the engine ensure that the handbrake is on, that is to say that the lever is pulled **up** to take the tension on the cable. This pulls the rear brake shoes onto the brake drums, ensuring that the vehicle will not move.

You must also make sure that the gear lever is in the neutral position. If a gear was selected and the engine was started with the clutch **up,** the vehicle would jump forward (or backwards if reverse gear was selected).

Remember that you can depress the clutch pedal quite quickly, but when you bring it back up it should be moved slowly, until you can feel the car trying to move away, this is called **biting point**. (The three factors of biting point are: 1. the engine noise will drop. 2. You will fell a slight vibration in the car. 3. The front of the car will rise up a little).

When **accelerating** (using more gas), this should be done by using gentle pressure with your **right** foot.

When **braking**, this should be done by using gentle pressure with your **right** foot. As you feel the vehicle slowing down you may increase the pressure on the pedal to allow the vehicle to slow down in a shorter distance, if required. When the vehicle is just about to stop, ease the pressure off the brake pedal (still maintaining a little pressure), to allow a smooth stop.

I am sure that you have been in a vehicle which, when it has come to a stop, you have felt yourself being thrown forward; this was due to the harsh amount of pressure being applied to the footbrake.

When slowing down to make a normal stop, think what is happening to your vehicle, you have selected a gear and the clutch pedal is **up**, this is sending a drive to the road wheels to move the vehicle. You are now pressing the footbrake pedal, which **will** make the vehicle stop. The brakes, on any vehicle is much stronger than the clutch, but as you are asking your car to both drive and stop, at slow speeds you will create a shudder through the vehicle. To avoid this and bring your vehicle to a smooth rest, the procedure is:

Slow the vehicle down gradually to around 4-5 miles per hour
Press the clutch down (keep it down)
Gently bring the vehicle to a halt (easing off the pressure on the brake pedal just before it actually stops).
Keep your feet still
Apply the handbrake
Select neutral
Cancel any signal given
Rest your feet

Clutch Control

In order to achieve, and maintain, good clutch control there are a few exercises that need to be mastered. Even before you start the engine it is possible to gain a little clutch control by simply pressing the clutch pedal down and slowly releasing the pressure until your foot is completely clear. (then practice changing through the gears, work your way from 1st through to 4th in sequence and then back down again).

The most effective method to ensure a smooth action is to press the heel of your shoe down onto the floor of the car, and bend your foot upwards from the ankle so that the pedal slides along the sole of your shoe, until the pedal has been completely released.

Once the engine has been started, you can then practice depressing the clutch and changing through the gears (make sure you keep the clutch pedal **down** during this exercise, and then work through the gears as above). When you have mastered this, continue to practice changing gears without looking down. Look straight ahead out of the windscreen. This is good practice for when the car is moving, as you will be watching where you are going rather than what you are doing.

When you are satisfied with this exercise the next stage is to move the car under full clutch control. By this I mean, that the only pedal you will use is the clutch pedal. Depress the clutch pedal and select 1st gear, slowly bring the clutch **up** to **biting point**, make your observations, and if safe to move off release the handbrake.

The car will move off very slowly, try bringing the clutch pedal up very slightly (about the thickness of a one pound coin), until the car moves a little faster. (the clutch pedal should be around half way up the full travel available).

Now the car is moving, depress the clutch pedal just a little (just below the biting point), until you feel the drive coming off the road wheels. Now that you have disconnected the drive from the road wheels, on a flat/level surface the vehicle will slow down and eventually come to rest. Just before your vehicle actually stops, slowly bring the clutch pedal back **up** to **biting point** and you will feel the vehicle being driven again. Repeat this as often as you can without letting the car actually stop.

Due to the very slow speed you will be driving, try this exercise on a long straight stretch of road, preferably with no other traffic around you. As you gain more control, practice this exercise on a slight gradient using a little gas. As you are now on a gradient you will need more power to move the vehicle uphill, so adjust the amount of gas you use to suit the severity of the gradient.

Gear Changing & Braking Exercise

As mentioned earlier in the gears section, when the gear lever is in the neutral position it will sit between 3rd and 4th gear. Use the palming method when using 1st and 2nd gear, and never rush changing gears.

At all times you will have to anticipate and assess when it would be appropriate to change gear, this takes practice, and your instructor will assist you by explaining about listening to the engine note, and gauging your speed. Basically, the gear should match the speed of the vehicle (see page 8).

To practice changing gears, from 1st gear, build your speed up to around 10mph, to 'move up' to 2nd gear, place your left hand on the gear lever (pressing gently to the left), then:

Press the clutch pedal down (keep it down), and at the same time
Off gas
Pull the gear lever straight back
Slowly clutch up (all the way)
Gentle pressure on the gas

(Remember to use the clutch and gas pedals like a see-saw, as the clutch goes down the gas comes up etc).

Braking Exercise

When using the footbrake you should always use gentle pressure as it will respond very quickly when applied. Always check your interior mirror, looking for following vehicles, before pressing the brake pedal, and look as far ahead as possible at all times to assess the road and conditions, as this will give advance warning of the possible need to slow down or stop.

To practice braking, build the road speed up to around 10mph (1st gear), and gently press the footbrake to bring the car to a halt. (Remember to press the clutch pedal down at around 4-5mph). Just as the vehicle is about to stop, ease the pressure off the footbrake (still applying a little pressure), so that your vehicle comes to a smooth rest. Once you have practiced this a few times build your speed up to 20mph and again bring your vehicle to a smooth halt.

Once you are comfortable at this speed, again increase the road speed to around 25-30mph and this time practice slowing the vehicle down to walking pace (5mph).

When you have reduced your speed you will then have to select a lower gear (probably 1st gear), and again build your speed up to 25-30mph and repeat the exercise until you achieve a 'feel' for the brake pedal.

Approaching Junctions (Turning Left & Right)

When approaching junctions to turn either left or right, the more information that we can collect on the approach, the safer the procedure becomes. As with everything we do in driving, forward planning and observation is essential to ensure our safety, and the safety of other road users.

The easiest junction to deal with is to turn left from a major road into a minor road, as you are going with the flow of traffic. For this briefing however, I will deal with turning left from a minor road into a major road. This junction can be recognised by both the road markings and advanced warning signs.

The procedure is:

Mirror
Check interior and nearside mirrors

Signal
Signal if it would help any other road user. As you are going to change direction it is always advisable to signal on the approach to any junction, as any vehicle entering or approaching the junction needs to know as soon as possible, the direction you intend to take.

Position
When turning left stay at your safety line (1 metre from the kerb), all the way round the junction (if safe to do so).

Speed
Slow the vehicle down by using progressive braking (rather than leaving it to the last minute), to the speed that would be safe to turn the corner at. As this junction is a give way, you should be prepared to

either give way or stop, so you should be slow enough to engage 1st gear about a car length before the give way markings.

Gear

The gear should match the speed of the car. Depending on how wide the junction is and how much of the new road you can see are additional factors to be considered. As a novice driver, it would be advisable to use 1st gear at a give way and if you are turning from a major road into a minor road without having to stop, possibly 2nd gear.

Look

The only time it is safe to enter or emerge from a junction is when you can see clearly in all directions.

If you can't see, don't go

Creep forward using clutch control, until you can see clearly and are positive that you can clear the junction safely. You may not move out if it would cause other road users to change speed or direction.

Emerging from Junctions

Before you emerge from any junction you have several decisions to make.

T. Junctions

Are there other vehicles approaching from the right or left?
Are they going to turn into your junction?
Do they intend to stop before your junction?
Are they going to cross your path?
What speed are they traveling?
Are there any pedestrians crossing the road, or intending to cross?
Is your vision restricted by parked cars, bends or hills?
Look out for cyclists especially if crossing a bus or cycle lane
Larger vehicles can sometimes hide other vehicle that are overtaking

You must not emerge from a junction if it would cause any other vehicle to change speed or direction and you must always give priority to pedestrians.

Y. Junctions

Y junctions are so called because you normally approach them from an angle, and as this may restrict your zone of vision for oncoming traffic, must be treated with great care.

When approaching a Y junction on the major road you should expect other vehicles to move onto the junction with you in their blind spot. You must always be prepared to slow down or stop if they continue onto the junction without seeing you.

When approaching a Y junction and **your** zone of vision is restricted you should: Approach as normal (page.17), and as you approach the junction, which is either a give way or an unmarked junction, steer your vehicle to the position of a **T** junction so that your vehicle is angled to give the best possible view into the junction. Move forward slowly using full clutch control, until you are sure you can clear the junction safely.

Crossroads

Particular attention has to be made to oncoming vehicles at crossroads. You will have to respond to whichever direction they take.

If **you** are turning right, you may be crossing the path of other vehicles and therefore must give way.
As with all junctions, once you have turned into the new road, check your mirrors so that you are aware of any following traffic.
Make progress if safe to do so.
Make sure your indicator has cancelled

INTERMEDIATE

CONGRATULATIONS!!!!!! You now have the basics of car control.

This next stage requires all the knowledge and control skills you have just mastered.

(If you are unsure of any element covered so far, continue to practice until you are confident you can safely move on to the next stage).

You will now be introduced to slightly busier roads and the routes will include a selection of all basic rule junctions i.e. Crossroads, Give Way and T junctions. You will also be introduced to Traffic Lights and Pedestrian Crossings and a varied selection of Uphill and Downhill gradients and roundabouts.

On the following pages you will find the lesson plans and main points for each lesson. You Instructor will give you a full briefing at the start of each lesson and will sketch a diagram to match your particular practice route and surroundings, which will allow you to study and recap each lesson and manoeuvre before your next lesson to ensure that you completely understand the lesson and achieve a positive outcome time after time.

Controls Lesson

Main Points

Doors, Seat (to include head restraint), Steering, Seatbelt, Mirrors.

Accelerator, Footbrake, Clutch.

Handbrake, Gears, Indicators and Starting Procedure.

Precautions before Moving Off, Normal Stop Position, Use of MSM, Normal Stop.

Move off / Normal Stop

Main Points

MSM routine, POM routine, Co-ordination of Controls, Normal Stop Position, Normal Stop Control.

Approaching Junctions to Turn Left or Right

Main Points

MSM routine, Braking, Gears, Coasting, Speed on Approach, Position, Pedestrians, Cross Approaching Traffic, Right Corner Cut.

Emerging from Junctions

Main Points

MSM routine, Speed, Gears, Coasting, Observation, Emerging, Position, Pedestrians.

Uphill and Downhill Starts

Main Points

MSM routine, POM routine, Power, Gears, Co-ordination

Emerging from Junctions

Main Points

MSM routine, Speed, Gears, Coasting, Observation, Emerging, Position, Pedestrians.

Uphill and Downhill Starts

Main Points

MSM routine, POM routine, Power, Gears, Co-ordination

Emergency Stops and Use of Mirrors

Main Points

Quick Reaction, Use of Footbrake and Clutch, Skidding, Mirrors (Vision and Use), Mirrors Direction, Overtaking, Stopping, MSM routine.

Straight Line Reverse

Main Points

Co-ordination of Controls, Observation, Accuracy.

Turn in the Road

Main Points

Co-ordination of the Controls, Observation, Accuracy.

Left Reverse

Main Points

Co-ordination of Controls, Observation, Accuracy.

Parallel Parking

Main Points

Co-ordination of Controls, Observation, Accuracy.

Crossroads

Main Points

MSM routine, Speed, Gears, Coasting, Observation, Emerging, Position, Pedestrians, Cross approaching Traffic, Right Corner Cut.

Pedestrian crossings and Use of Mirrors

Main Points

MSN routine, Speed on Approach, Stop when Necessary, Overtaking on Approach, Inviting Pedestrians to Cross, Signals by Indicator, Arm Signals, Signal Timing, Unnecessary Signals.

Progress / Hesitancy and Normal Stops

Main Points

Progress too Fast, Progress too Slow, Hesitancy, Normal Position too wide from the Left / too Close to the Left.

Meet, cross and overtake other Traffic

(Allowing adequate clearance for other road users, and anticipation)

Main Points

MSM routine, Meet Approaching Traffic, Overtake other Traffic, Keep a Safe Distance, Shaving other Vehicles, Anticipation of Pedestrians / Cyclists and other Drivers.

Making Progress

A this stage of driver training you should have a good understanding of what is required of you to pass the practical element of the DSA Driving Test. By now you will have mastered the control aspect of your vehicle, and in making progress you will demonstrate several additional skills which the examiner will be looking for.

What is required, is that you can make reasonable progress when driving the route chosen for your test, driving at speeds suitable to both road and traffic conditions. You will also be expected to move off from junctions as soon as it is safe to do so. An empty road can only get busy, so if there are no vehicles or other road users, believe what you see and **make progress.**

Unlike other aspects of the driving test, there is no special exercise where you can demonstrate making progress, it is continually assessed during your drive, so make sure that you show confidence and good judgement, comply with speed limits and keep up with the flow of traffic.

Driving too slowly which may hold up traffic, being over cautious when approaching junctions and waiting when it is safe to move off are all errors to be avoided. You driving lessons should by now, be conducted on roads and traffic density to allow you to practice this aspect of driving ability.

Good observation and forward planning are now required to allow you time to achieve the correct speed with regard to:

The type of road

Type and density of traffic

Weather and visibility

The following page shows a complete breakdown of the Officially Recommended Syllabus for the DSA Driving Test. You will have to demonstrate, Skill, Knowledge and Understanding in all areas (if appropriate), in order to pass the test.

Your Driving Instructor has the knowledge and experience to know when you are ready for the test (and what is expected of you). Learners who pass first time do so because they are well instructed, have plenty of practice, and wait until they are ready. Attempting the test before your instructor confirms that you are ready, often results in failure and additional expense.

officially Recommended Syllabus

1. Show me, tell me Questions
2. Take proper precautions before getting in or out of the vehicle
3. Safety checks before starting the engine: DSSSM routine, Handbrake applied and Gear Lever in the neutral position
4. Start the engine and move off straight ahead and at an angle—on a level road, uphill and downhill
5. Select the correct road position for normal driving
6. Use proper observation in all traffic conditions
7. Drive at a speed suitable for road and traffic conditions
8. React promptly to all risks
9. Change traffic lanes
10. Pass stationary vehicles
11. Meet, overtake, and cross the path of other vehicles
12. Turn right and left at junctions, including crossroads and roundabouts
13. Drive ahead at crossroads and roundabouts
14. Keep a safe separation distance when following other vehicles
15. Act correctly at pedestrian crossings
16. Show proper regard for the safety of other road users
17. Drive on both urban and rural roads, and where possible dual carriageways
18. Comply with traffic signals given by police, traffic wardens, and other road users
19. Stop the vehicle safely, normally and in an emergency, without locking the wheels

20. Turn in the road exercise, reverse into a side road, Parallel Park the vehicle
21. Park the vehicle in a parking bay in forward and/or reverse gears
22. Cross all types of railway level crossing

Pass Plus

The Pass plus Scheme, operated by many driving instructors, is a training scheme linked to insurance discounts that will benefit all newly qualified drivers by:

Saving you money on your car insurance

Showing you a positive driving style which is both enjoyable and safe

Helping you gain quality driving experience safely

The Pass Plus scheme has been developed by the Department for Transport (DfT), local Government and the Regions, with the help of insurers and the Driving Instruction Industry. The scheme has been developed to:

Improve your skills in areas where you may have little experience

Reduce your risk of being involved in a road accident

You will have to pay for your course but, if you complete it successfully, you will be offered a discount on your car insurance by one of the companies taking part in the scheme. The precise saving will depend on the company you choose. Fees for the Pass Plus course vary depending on where you live and the instructor or driving school you choose. By taking part in the scheme you are demonstrating that you want to be a skilful and responsible driver.

The aim of the Pass Plus Scheme

The Pass Plus Scheme will:

Speed up the process of gaining good driving experience

Teach you positive driving skills. Throughout the course you will be driving with two key factors in mind:

Attitude
Responsibility for your actions
Care and consideration for others

Skills
Observation
Assessing what you see
Making decisions
Taking the correct action

Your instructor will tell you why they are the key to a positive driving style

Additional Topics and Useful Tips for Qualified Drivers

Attitudes

Cockpit Drills

Observations

Speed & Safety

Acceleration and Braking

Positioning

Steering and Reversing

Skidding

Signals

Road Signs and Markings

Overtaking

Motorway Driving

Types of Crossings

Questions & Answers about ABS

Attitudes

Mental

Emotional upsets affect concentration and driving i.e. recent family upsets

Tolerance, understanding and consideration for other road users are required to be a good driver

Recognise your own limitations and don't drive beyond them

Aggressive behaviour on the road stems from a disregard for social values

Delays can cause frustration and stress. Allow plenty of time for journeys

Risks

RTA's account for half of all accidental deaths in the U.K. and a quarter of all adult deaths under 30years of age, and the largest single cause of death and injury for young adults

Human error is the cause of 90% of RTA's. (How often have you heard that 'fog caused a motorway pile-up', well, fog never caused any such thing, bad driving did.

All drivers have a one in seven chance of being in an accident

Characteristics of a good driver

Accurate observations, attention, and awareness of risks

Speed and direction according to road and weather conditions

Knowing the limitations of both yourself and your vehicle

Skilful use of the vehicle controls

Alertness

Anxiety, tiredness and monotony all affect alertness
Scan the whole area of vision, not just the tunnel in front of you
Look for hazards of all shapes, sizes and directions
Expect hazards in particular situations, and expect the unexpected

Skills

Learn from experience. Continue to assess your attitude to driving and other road users

Every near miss should be seen as an opportunity to re-evaluate and improve your technique

Critical self awareness and acceptance of your vulnerability should be maintained

Do not do anything that forces another road user to brake, accelerate or change direction

Red Mist

A phenomenon known to the authorities before 'Road Rage' hit the headlines. A state of mind of the driver who is determined to achieve a goal at any cost, and is no longer capable of assessing risks. They have become emotionally and physiologically caught up in the chase. They ignore risk factors such as weather conditions and other traffic etc.

Self discipline, stay calm, avoid personality conflict with other road users, and concentration, are ways to avoid Red Mist.

Cockpit Drill

Vehicle Type

The vehicle you drive at work may not be the vehicle you drove to work, and you might not be the driver who last used that particular vehicle. Also consider what type of vehicle you are now going to drive i.e. Van, LGV, and PCV etc. Is the gear change a standard 'H' or something different, (a four wheel drive, split box, automatic).
Are all doors secured including any rear or side doors.
What are the speed restrictions for this vehicle?
Are there any other legal requirements (Have you complied with them)?

Position

Adjust seat to ensure good all round vision and access to controls, adjusting steering wheel if appropriate, seat belt, mirrors, especially exterior mirrors, before moving off.
Do not use a mobile phone when driving.

Controls

Does the parking brake work! TRY IT
Is the indicator stalk on the right or left hand side of the steering column?
Where is the control for lights, horn etc?
Check all indication (warning) lights are working when you turn on the ignition, and note that most extinguish when the engine starts
Prove brakes are effective as soon as possible after moving off. Remember to check your interior mirror before braking

Power

Petrol (fuel) . . . Oil . . . . Water . . . . Electrics (indicators and brake lights) . . . Rubber . . . (Tyres and Wipers), should all be checked before starting any journey.

Size

Is this vehicle longer, taller, wider, than your own or usual vehicle
The turning radius may be greater, don't allow the rear end cut corners or mount the kerb
Check the vision in this vehicle is it more or less than usual. Make allowances, you can use reflections in shop windows to help you gauge the length/distance
If a gap doesn't look large enough it probably isn't

observations

Using Senses

Use sight, hearing and even smell to gain information about conditions

Look as far ahead as possible and scan both sides of the road, focus to the distance, middle distance and near to you, alternate your mirror checks to accommodate the area behind your vehicle

If you play your music too loud you won't hear horns or sirens

Planning

A good driving plan puts you in the correct position, at the right speed, at the right time to negotiate hazards. As conditions change, plan changes.

The Plan: Observe—Anticipate—Prioritise—Decide

Anticipation

Anticipating hazards gives you extra time to react to them

Good observation assists anticipation

Allow for other peoples mistakes

Place hazards in order of importance

Hazards

Hazards are: anything that is potentially dangerous, either moving or stationary

Look for what is around the next bend, if you can't see . . . . . . .SLOW DOWN

Weather

Mostly obvious, but remember, use lights in bad visibility, but NOT rear fog lights in rain or when visibility is more than 100 metres

Only use fog lights in fog or falling snow

Wet and ice patches linger in the shade of trees in early morning

Beware patchy fog

Observation Links

(Clues to the likely behaviour of other road users)

Parked vehicles can mean doors may open, people stepping out, or a vehicle pulling out in front of you. (From either side).

Fresh mud on the road can mean a slow moving tractor ahead, or slippery road

An accident could cause other drivers to slow down to have a look . . . Rubber Neckers

A cluster of lamp posts in the distance: possibly a roundabout ahead or junction

No gap in a line of trees ahead: road may bend to the left or right

Build up your own library of links, as you gain more driving experience you will Observe, Anticipate, Prioritise and Decide well in advance.

Speed and Safety

Limits

Know and obey national speed limits
Drive within your own competence
Always drive knowing that you are able to stop within the distance you can see, especially at night
Speed perception is different inbuilt up areas, to that of an open road

Vehicle

Know the limits of the vehicle you are driving, with or without a trailer
When driving an unfamiliar vehicle, allow time to adjust to it. Get used to how it reacts to controls etc
Keep an eye on the speedometer when driving a different vehicle, some vehicles respond quicker than others

Stopping Distances

If you double your speed you quadruple your stopping distance. (More in adverse weather conditions)
The condition of your vehicle will also affect your stopping distance i.e. shock absorbers, tyres etc. Check them

Weather and Road Conditions

Always slow down when driving in rain, snow, fog, ice, high winds etc
The National speed limit is not always a safe speed limit, assess the conditions and drive accordingly

Comfort

Think f the comfort of yourself and your passengers. Don't race round corners and bends, brake suddenly, or accelerate harshly. If it feels fast it probably is **Too Fast.**

Acceleration and Braking

Correct Gear

Always match the gear to the road speed

The correct gear ensures good control, smooth acceleration, and saves wear & tear on the engine and gearbox

In modern vehicles with relatively high ratio gear boxes, try using 5th gear at 50mph and above, 4th in a 40mph zone, and 3rd in a 30mph speed limit, and so on. This offers excellent control in built up areas, and gives no higher fuel consumption than if you floor the accelerator in high gear. (Excluding low ratio vans and Lorries etc).

Type of Vehicle

Remind yourself of the vehicle you are driving. I.e. Standard Gear Box, 4 x 4, Automatic!

Get used to the feel and response of the change of vehicle, and avoid jerky use of all controls

Consider the braking system. Is it conventional hydraulic brakes or air brakes!

Acceleration Sense

Develop the ability to vary the vehicle speed according to the conditions by use of the accelerator only. This requires careful observations, anticipation, and good judgement of speed and distance of other vehicles and hazards

Good acceleration sense avoids the need for unnecessary or harsh braking

Cadence Braking

Repeated on/off application of the footbrake to avoid skidding
Brakes are at their most efficient just before they lock
ABS does this for you now, but is no substitute for bad driving

Handbrake

Only to be used when stationary
Don't 'ratchet up' the handbrake, use the release button. (Be car friendly)
At every stop of more than a few seconds, get into the habit of applying the handbrake and selecting neutral. Brake lights at night and in the rain dazzle following drivers

Corners and Hazards

Don't change gear half way round a corner. It de-stabilises the vehicle and you have to take a hand off the steering wheel when you need it most. (Forward Plan).
Do not accelerate into corners or other hazards. Decelerate or brake before, and accelerate away, if safe to do so

Positioning

Lane Discipline

The ideal road position depends on: Safety, Observations, Conditions, and manoeuvrability

Safety Zone: a position roughly midway between nearside hazards, like pedestrians, cyclists, parked cars etc, and offside hazards, oncoming traffic

Don't keep changing lanes to gain time in queues of traffic. Choose the correct lane for the direction you intend to take on approach and stay with it.

Pull into nearside lane after overtaking, if safe to do so. Especially on Motorways

Left Hand Bends

Approach slightly to the right of your lane to obtain a better view of the road ahead, this also helps you avoid cutting corners or mounting the kerb with large vehicles

Right Hand Bends

Approach slightly left of centre to obtain the best view, which also helps to avoid cutting corners and straying into oncoming traffic

Following Large Vehicles

Keep back. Your view will be much better on both sides, and you will then be able to see any hand signals given.

Remember—If you cannot see their mirrors, they cannot see you

Keeping a safe distance from large vehicles avoids too mush spray and other debris thrown up from tyres

Parking / Stopping

Park safely. Do not park near hazards, or on the opposite side of the road facing oncoming traffic

Don't stop too close behind the vehicle in front, leave room to pull out and pass should it break down or be unable to move. Remember the rule: when you stop behind a vehicle, you should be able to see their tyres on the road. (This leaves around half a car length which is enough room to manoeuvre if required).

Leaving this gap also helps to prevent you from being shunted into the vehicle if you are shunted by a following vehicle

Steering and Reversing

Method

Use the Pull-Push method when steering
Don't hold the steering wheel too tightly, but tighten your grip when circumstances dictate
Keep both hands on the steering wheel at all times, except when using the controls or making hand signals
Do not use a mobile phone (either hand held or hands free) when driving, this will affect your concentration level

Position

Adjust your seat and steering wheel for comfort. Uncomfortable driving positions causes fatigue etc, and hold the wheel at 'Ten to two' or 'quarter to three' position
Approach left hand bends slightly to the right of your lane, and for right hand bends slightly to the left of your lane in order to improve your zone of vision
Use the limit point to assist you. This is the furthest point along the road you can see, and you must be able to stop within this distance.
The 'Limit Point' is at its minimum going into a bend, but increases as you come out of it

Speed

Different vehicles can corner at different speeds. Know your vehicle and drive accordingly
Steering is heavier at low speeds and lighter at high speeds. Power steering will even out the effort required, but does not prevent

over-steer or under-steer if your vehicle speed is not matched to conditions and severity of bends and corners

The wear on tyres is more pronounced when cornering at speed, as they overcome the vehicle natural tendency to carry on in a straight line

Reversing

Reversing accounts for around 30% of Company vehicle accidents

Scan all around and observe before reversing. Use mirrors but be aware of blind spots

If you cannot see clearly behind, ask someone to guide you, if there is no-one nearby get out of the vehicle and have a look yourself.

Always reverse slowly. Never faster than walking pace

Vehicles behave erratically when driven at speed in reverse

When reverse parking, remember the front of your vehicle will move out further into the road

Do not reverse into major roads or around blind corners

Forces

Be aware of the forces affecting your vehicles ability to corner safely, a moving vehicle naturally wants to continue in a straight line, as do its passengers

As acceleration and braking tend to throw the weight of your vehicle backwards and forwards respectively, so cornering throws the weight of your vehicle away from the direction of bends, thereby de-stabilising it, particularly high sided vehicles. Learn to recognise over-steer and under-steer, it is a characteristic of the vehicle itself and varies between front wheel drive and rear wheel drive.

FWD vehicles under-steer and RWD over-steer

Skidding

Avoidance

Drive safely within the limits of: Conditions, your Vehicle, and Yourself

Every skid is different and all vehicles respond in a different way. **Know your vehicle**

Skids are caused by sudden or involuntary changes in speed or direction

Ice and snow **do not** cause skidding, driving without regard for the conditions do

Good observations, Anticipation, Planning and Technique will help avoid skids

ABS / Traction Control

ABS is basically a mechanised cadence braking system. It releases the brakes just as the wheels are about to loch-up. It doesn't prevent skidding, in some cases it can exacerbate the problem.

On a good, dry surface it can reduce the stopping distance of your vehicle, but if you activate the ABS, then you were not observing, anticipating or planning in the first place, and that won't help the vehicle behind you which may not be fitted with ABS.

Traction systems adjust the engine power to the driving wheels according to slip. Each

System is different, so you should consult the handbook for each vehicle driven

Front Wheel Skids

The vehicle continues in a straight line when you turn the steering wheel

Remove the cause, which is usually excess speed. I.e. release the accelerator, or steer into the skid until the road wheel grip is re-gained, and then steer out of the skid

Rear Wheel Skid

The rear of the vehicle tends to swing out to the outside of the bend

Remove the cause, usually speed again, and gently steer into the skid until the grip is re-gained, then re-apply the steering in the desired direction and re-apply power

Four Wheel Skids

Usually caused by harsh braking, allowing the wheels to 'lock-up'.

Release the brakes, (not ABS), release the accelerator

Re-gain steering control and gently apply power

Signals

Purpose

To inform others of your presence or intentions
Only give a signal when another road user will benefit from it
Always make clear, unambiguous signals

Types

Hand signals
Indicators, horn, hazard lights, brake lights and headlights
Courtesy signals
Be wary of signals from people other than officials, and always check that it is safe to proceed yourself

Use Of

Always make sure your signals are cancelled after use
Use the horn to notify others of your presence, not as a rebuke
Only use hazard warning lights when you have stopped, or to warn others. **Not** when you are going into a shop

Headlights

Can be used as an alternative to the horn a night
A headlight flash is not an invitation to proceed
Flash headlights at night to warn others of your presence on the approach to bends, hump back bridge, or prior to overtaking

Courtesy

Raise your hand or palm by way of a thank you, or nod your head

Do not place the control of your vehicle at risk

Road Signs and Markings

Highway Code

Be familiar with all road signs and markings in the current edition
Also make use of unofficial signs, such as, 'Mud on the Road', 'Car Boot Sale' etc
Posts with multi-signs should be read from the top down, which allows you to prioritise the hazards in sequence

Orders

Mostly circular with a red border, i.e. Speed Limit, No Overtaking, Width or Weight Limit signs, with the exception of 'Give Way'.
Blue circles no border give positive instruction i.e. Turn Left, Minimum Speed Limit etc

Warning

Mostly Triangular with a red border i.e. Road Narrows, Two Way Traffic, Bend to the Left / Right, Low Flying Aircraft!!!!!

Direction

Mostly rectangular
Blue background for Motorways
Green background for primary routes
Black borders for non-primary routes
Information signs are all rectangular i.e. One Way Street, Countdown Markers

Markings (Road & Vehicle)

Across Carriageways, 'Give Way', 'Stop Line'.
Along Carriageways, 'Double White Lines', 'Cross Hatching'.
Edge of Carriageway, 'Yellow Lines'.
LGV Markings, 'Long Vehicle' etc
Hazard Plates, 'Chemicals'.

overtaking

Hazards

Consider the vehicle you overtake, if stationary doors may open, you may swerve as you pass if you're not prepared
Oncoming vehicles
Junctions and bends
Parked vehicles
Overtaking a line of traffic, don't move from lane to lane to queue jump
Do not overtake at or near, junctions, schools, hospitals, roundabouts, level crossings or at the brow of a hill

Stationary Vehicles

Relatively straightforward, as is passing slow moving vehicles. Remember 'Forward Planning and Anticipation'
Remember your observation links; try to leave doors width between you and other vehicles
Consider your speed on approach and anticipate other road users, particularly pedestrians

Moving Vehicles

Consider the acceleration capabilities of your vehicle, and the relative speed of other vehicle around you
Always leave yourself somewhere to go if you have to abort the manoeuvre
Use vision limit points wherever possible
Remember. On single carriageway roads, you are in the danger zone

Method / Technique

Approach—Follow—Overtaking Position—Overtake—and resume normal road position

Identify the hazard i.e. One vehicle, two, three vehicles to overtake!!!

Assess relative speeds and road markings

Select the gear which delivers the maximum acceleration—close up to the vehicle to be overtaken (not too close to obscure your vision)—re-assess conditions (following traffic, and speeds etc), then carry out the manoeuvre as quickly as possible

Motorway Driving

Conditions

Assess traffic density on approach, from slip road (acceleration lane) or fly-over, look for any road works, lane closures or possible LGV's in convoy which may block you joining the motorway

Assess your own physical condition: Tired, Unwell or Stressed

Assess the condition of your vehicle

Joining

Do not overtake on a slip road, unless you are overtaking a slow moving LGV and can see clearly that you have plenty of room, time and distance to do so safely

Look as far ahead as possible, look for a suitable gap in the traffic flow, and as you are about to emerge look over your right shoulder to ensure there are no vehicles in your blind spot

Be prepared to stop if necessary. These white lines are 'Give Way' lines, don't just barge out and force other to change speed or direction

Lane Discipline

You should always be in the left hand lane unless overtaking

Signal in good time, complete the overtake, then: Mirror, signal, and move back in. DO NOT HOG THE MIDDLE OR OUTSIDE LANES

Regularly monitor your instruments, road signs and other traffic

Keep alert. Open the windows a little (even when raining), to keep fresh air circulating and take regular breaks on long journeys

Watch out for fast moving traffic joining the motorway, and be prepared to move over to the next lane (if safe to do so). Should they force their way in be prepares to slow down and leave a suitable safety gap

Leaving

PLAN AHEAD

Look for advanced warning signs and get yourself into the appropriate lane in plenty of time. DO NOT cut across lanes at the last minute to exit the motorway

Weather

Any inclement weather is usually magnified on exposed stretches of motorway

Rain will cause spray and poor visibility, particularly from Lorries and buses

Be prepared for black ice. Fog is more prevalent and the sun can blind your vision

Patchy fog is very dangerous at higher motorway speeds, and as discussed earlier, 'Fog never caused a crash, bad driving did'.

Watch for diesel spillage and other debris on the motorway

Cross-winds are more of a problem on the motorway, beware the slipstreams of LGV's and Buses, and leave as much room as possible when overtaking large vehicles as they can be affected by high winds

Types of crossings

Pedestrian crossings fall into two categories. The first being 'Controlled Crossings', include:
Pelican, Puffin, and Toucan, and use traffic signals to control the flow of traffic. The second category is 'Uncontrolled Crossings', these include: Zebra Crossings and Pedestrian Refuges.

Controlled Crossings Pelican

The pelican crossing is a pedestrian light controlled crossing. Pelicans are activated by pedestrians when they push the button on the wait box. Pedestrians need to make sure that all traffic has stopped before they cross, and only when the green man has lit up. Pedestrians should not cross if the green man is flashing. There is also a bleeper which operates at the same time as the green man for blind and partially sighted pedestrians.

Puffin

The Puffin crossing is a '**P**edestrian **U**ser **F**riendly **In**telligent Crossing. These crossings are similar to Pelican crossings and activated in the same way by pedestrians. The main difference between the two crossings is that the RED and GREEN signals are above the wait box and not across the other side of the road. Puffins also have sensors built in which can detect pedestrians waiting, and make sure that the vehicle traffic remains stationary until they have crossed the road.

Toucan

The Toucan crossing or **'Two-Can'** crossing is a dual use crossing for both pedestrians and cyclists. The crossing is activated by a button on the wait box in much the same way as the Pelican and Puffin crossings. Toucans are sited where cycle routes cross roads, and cyclists do not have to dismount to cross at these points. The Toucan crossing has a **Green** and **Red** cyclist as well as Green and Red man as signals. Toucans are operated by sensors, and drivers must wait for a GREEN light before proceeding.

Uncontrolled Crossing Zebra

Zebra crossings consist of thick black and white strips across a road, with an orange flashing beacon on either pavement. These crossings give pedestrians priority; however, they must make sure that all traffic has stopped before using the crossing.

Pedestrian Refuges

Pedestrian refuges or traffic islands are place in the middle of wider roads where there is no crossing point. This helps to narrow the road, giving pedestrians a safe area, whilst they wait to cross the other half of the road. **Drivers** have priority at traffic islands.

Questions and Answers about ABS

What is ABS?

ABS is an acronym for anti-lock braking system, one of the most significant safety advances in automotive engineering in recent decades. First developed and patented in 1936, ABS is actually derived from the German term 'antiblockiersystem'.

Anti-lock brakes are designed to prevent skidding and help drivers maintain steering control during an emergency stopping situation. In cars equipped with conventional brakes, the driver pumps the brakes, whereas in cars equipped with four-wheel ABS, the driver keeps a firm foot on the brake, allowing the system to rapidly and automatically pump the brakes. Because the wheels don't lock drivers have the ability to steer around hazards if they are unable to stop in time.

What does ABS do for me?

ABS can improve vehicle stability, steer ability and stopping capability.

When the braking force created by the driver is greater than the tyre can handle, the wheel can lock-up. Locked wheels can create vehicle instability and prevent steering around obstacles in the road. Stopping distance on many slippery surfaces will also increase with locked wheels. Four-wheel ABS pre vents wheel lock-up in situations in which the wheels might normally lock, such as on slippery roads.

ABS can also prevent tyre damage. Locked wheels on dry asphalt or concrete can quickly create flat spots on tyres, which can cause an annoying vibration while driving. The big advantage, however, is the maintenance of the tyre—a significant factor in effective stopping.

Most anti-lock brake systems will indicate their operation by pulsations in the brake pedal and a noticeable sound. If the driver notices these pulsations and sounds, it is an indication that the roads are slippery. Speed and following distance should therefore be adjusted.

To reap the maximum safety benefits of ABS, drivers must know how to use the system correctly.

How does it work?

In vehicles equipped with conventional brakes, drivers often apply their brakes to the point at which the wheels lock up. This results in a loss of steering control and less-than-maximum braking effect.

When a driver operating a four-wheel ABS-equipped vehicle steps firmly on the brake pedal, the system automatically modulates the brake pressure at all four wheels, adjusting pressure to each wheel independently to prevent wheel lock-up.

With ABS, stopping distances decrease in many cases and the driver can maintain steering control of the vehicle. Importantly, four-wheel ABS allows the driver continuing control to help steer around hazards if a complete stop cannot be accomplished in time.

How do you know your ABS is working?

Most anti-lock brake systems let you know when you have activated your ABS. The driver usually notices a mechanical sound and can feel some pulsation or increased resistance to the brake pedal. This means traction limits have been reached on the road being travelled. It is important not to take your foot off the brake pedal when you hear noise or feel vibrations, but instead continue to apply firm pressure.

What is the difference between rear-wheel anti-locks (RWAL) and four-wheel anti-locks?

Rear-wheel anti-lock brakes (RWAL), found exclusively on light trucks, vans and sports utility vehicles, and are designed to maintain directional stability. Four-wheel anti-lock brakes, usually found on passenger cars and some light trucks, are designed to maintain steer ability in emergency stopping situations.

Because the braking system in a four-wheel anti-lock vehicle modulates the braking pressure and thereby prevents wheel lock on all four wheels, the driver maintains control over steering. Drivers of RWAL vehicles, on the other hand, control the braking and thus the lock prevention capabilities of the front wheels. If the driver steps too firmly on the brake pedal, the front wheels can lock and prevent steering . . . .

The same that would happen with conventional brakes. But with RWAL ABS, the vehicle continues to move in a straight line. With just enough pressure applied, the driver with RWAL can maintain steering control.

Drivers with four-wheel ABS cars should step firmly on the brake in an emergency stopping situation and keep their foot on the pedal. Drivers with RWAL vehicles should step firmly with care, and if they feel the wheels begin to lock, they should withhold some pressure.

Do cars with ABS stop more quickly than cars without it?

Not always. Although the stopping distance with ABS is shorter under most road conditions, drivers should always keep a safe distance behind the vehicle in front of them and maintain a speed consistent with the road conditions. While a vehicle with ABS maintains its steering capability in a sudden stop, it may not turn as quickly on a slippery road as it would on a dry surface.

Can you loose steer ability

The tyre can deliver a fixed amount of traction for the road conditions. This traction is divided between steering and braking. A driver can continue to steer a vehicle using maximum ABS braking, but not as sharply as he or she could without braking.

Can ABS stop all car skids?

While ABS cannot prevent all skids, it does prevent the wheel from locking in typical panic situations. ABS cannot, however, change the laws of physics. A combination of excessive speed, sharp turns and slamming brakes can still throw an ABS-equipped vehicle into a sideways skid.

In what circumstances might conventional brakes have an advantage over ABS

There are some conditions where stopping distance may be shorter without ABS. For example, in cases where the road is covered with loose gravel or freshly fallen snow, the locked wheels of a non-ABS car build up a wedge of gravel or snow, which can contribute to a shortening of the braking distance.

If I live in the Snow Belt, how can I benefit from ABS?

Even in fresh snow conditions, you gain the advantages of better steer ability and stability with four-wheel ABS than with a conventional system that could result in locked wheels.

In exchange for an increased stopping distance, the vehicle will remain stable and maintain full steering since the wheels won't be locked. The gain in stability makes a potential increase in stopping distances an acceptable compromise for most drivers. All in all, these benefits outweigh the rare instances where the ABS system increases distances over non-ABS equipped vehicles.

Does ABS work on ice?

Yes. The systems computer monitors the speed of each of the vehicles wheels, compares them, and adjusts brake pressure to each wheel to ensure the car stops in the shortest distance possible for most road surfaces.

Will pumping the brakes on ABS-equipped vehicles improve braking performance?

No. When in use, the ABS automatically varies the brake pressure much better than pumping can. Do not pump the brakes; apply firm pressure.

What if ABS fails

Anti-lock brake systems are designed to be fail-safe. Nevertheless, they are equipped with a diagnostic feature that automatically activates and tests major components each time the car is started, and monitors them throughout the journey. In the rare event of a failure, the ABS would be deactivated by its own safety circuit. A warning light goes on indicating to the driver that the vehicle is now in conventional base-brake mode. (See cockpit drill & ignition).

Why invest in a system you may use only a few times

When you consider that ABS can protect your automotive investment, your health and safety, passengers and other motorists, ABS is a good investment. Most people agree the investment in ABS proves its worth if it prevents just one accident. Maybe that's why nearly nine out of ten first-time buyers in Europe are repeat buyers.

How do you know if the vehicle I'm driving has ABS?

Most new car models offer ABS as either standard or optional equipment. There are different ways to find out whether your car has an anti-lock brake system:

If you buy or lease a new car, ask your dealer

Check your instrument panel for an ABS indicator light after you turn on the ignition

Read your owners manual

If renting a vehicle, check with the rental company when picking it up

Read the owners manual

Ask the dealer

If you buy or lease a new vehicle, check the window sticker equipment listing

A qualified mechanic can tell you by checking under the bonnet to determine if your vehicle has rear wheel anti-lock brakes or four wheel ABS: and reviewing the brake hose routings and ABS package.

This section is not exhaustive, but hopefully it has answered most of the questions you may have relating to Anti-Lock Braking Systems.

It is my intention that the information within this book steers you towards safe driving and success in your driving test.

Moving a vehicle is the easy part, forward planning and observation are the attributes that make a safe driver

Good Luck and Safe Driving for Life

Peter Gilpin

www.ingramcontent.com/pod-product-compliance
Lightning Source LLC
Chambersburg PA
CBHW020338290526
45785CB00005B/2069

9781456841775